CHEERLEADERS AND STRAIGHTJACKETS

A Journey Through Psychosis

"The Hospital Arrest"

BY: Miranda Dye Nehus

Part Two – Almost Four Years Later

"The Hospital Arrest"

The Billings Clinic Psych ER and Center became such a huge part of my psychosis. I would go there to play with Jake. He was always waiting for me there, breathing in the walls...breathing in and out opposite of me, as I revive him from the dead. I'd sing at the top of my lungs, songs that came into my being...from Sheryl Crow, to Zombie...Somewhere Over the Rainbow, was a big one, but I always had a ton of songs that would come into my head. Popping up from word associations. I was performing for the spirit world and felt so famous...rivalling Angelina Jolie in actress skills, I would do all kinds of voices and holler and make a big deal of myself. I often thought my army of men were on the floor, and the floor would even wiggle around like little ant men crawling. The baseboard of the room became a movie strip, and I could lay on my mattress watching in detail the storyline that gets created in my head, for all that I am telling you. Every time I went to the hospital I would heavily hallucinate.

I can trade places with objects and people when I am like this. I do a pattern of movement and intended outcome being that I meet up with Jake's soul. It wasn't always about Jake but ultimately led to him. In 2013 it was definitely about "Adam" Fox! I had needed to pack some items that were a part of my heritage, and I needed a soul mate in order to cross over to heaven. It was like that in four previous demonic and intense psychoses, I only had four over a period of 16 years. This is fully described in my first book, "Fairytale of Felony Stalker, A Memoir of Early Sobriety," written in 2013. August of 2013, ended up with me talking to God in my mother's womb, as she sat next to me in the ER. He said "this time, don't come out screaming for your father!" He told me a lot of things, actually, while I was in the womb, but I most recall, my God hole is about men, that I in fact was always missing that piece of having a father. But this time I would be born again and know I could be whole without a father. I symbolically broke my mom's water by throwing it on the ground, I said "I am ready, let me out! I won't forget this time." Of course, I was to be married in the spirit world, and of course it was Adam. I had never been so thrilled...I had found a soul mate! I wasn't going to be a germ at the bottom hell anymore, and my life played in a reel backwards. It was so funny to watch all my bloopers and misconceptions turn into comedy, as what had seemed like doom, was all actually in my favor. My dreams often play out in horrible scenes but will loop back for good. A peculiar twist in perception, but we know that God works all things for good for those that love him. That was my time, that was my day, and we were all gloriously crossed over as one. I stayed like that for a month, in a heavenly realm, and texted Adam 7 times in the month of August, after a restraining order.

The faces of the Psych staff always morph, and shift and I can see them changing right before my eyes. My theory for that is that they are trading quality female traits with male traits and vice versa. The trading goes back to the beginning of time, and we all have lineage. It is based on genetic inheritance of what would someday be considered beautiful or not. Like asking a brother if he would trade his sister for being short...who wants the dark hair? Who wants this pointy nose? The left eye crossed? That was always a big deal to me to see a cross-eye. It indicated a transfer. In this realm and by this time everyone is beautiful. There was an Australian woman who worked the ER, and I always was so stunned by Jaime's appearance. She was a Goddess to me. Tall and dark. I think I come into this Eutopia where we are all whole and beautiful in our own right. There is no deformity in this realm...we are all healthy. Trading an ailment for a cure. I trade down to the last cell of my being, which is why I often keep my clothes off in the ER, I have traded every piece of clothing, or item I had in my purse (which is always documented). I believe that I had to trade places with Jake's death somehow and that he is resurrecting from the dead. We are simply exchanging clothes. And I could play any role in the

ER. Hell, I was a doctor! I was the nurse, I was the police officer…all clothes come into the ER, but we come out naked like when we are born and have to exchange with people. I once showed up to the ER with food in a tote, and three little glass penguins. I'd tried everything to see Jake and I thought they had given me so much free food, I need to come bearing gifts. The glass penguins represented black and white, yin and yang. I think that people walk into the ER, the old and the sick die…and then boom a baby is born in out of the spirit world. That we are all just coming and going in rides. Taking turns coming in and out the Reincarnation HUB, the Billings Clinic.

Standing in line for pills in psych. I learned the order of ABC's. Spelling of names and birth orders also in the lockdown area. Like a splice in time, I could be any person. Or even control clocks. Still all the trading for traits, whether that even be for good qualities in personality. Trust I can trade anything spiritually to get what I want. Food is a big deal. The order of the way food is offered and delivered. I often save food for my soul mate. I share it with him! I portion out my food to share with my ghost!

It all goes back to Seattle. October 1st, 1978. The Space Needle had been built in my family's honor. I get so big in my mind that it becomes just a symbol of my power in my birth place. Or that I am a beacon on the tip of the Space Needle, and every shot I take is for the glory of reincarnated souls. It was foretold that I would be injected with an ailment at birth. A schizophrenic code. A wiring of genetics not so uncommon in the population, as it had been discovered by the Nazi's in all their experiments to recreate the Nephalim. Something that would assimilate illness in my later life, which would not be triggered until I was older. This is how I know babies talk in the nurseries. They were just there before birth. I mean they were alive in utero, but it was in preparation to be brought out to the war on earth. Souls diving into bodies fully at the crown of birth. My mother gave birth to me at the University Hospital on a Sunday. There were students watching her, how uncomfortable! Then they whisked me away and injected my life's curve ball. I believe they have done this to billions of people who are in this spiritual game. I also believe I was chosen to be a leader in the war, due to my birth order and inheritance of a genetic nature. I am a Queen in this reality, ConCord. Born to be fierce and a warrioress, that defends the realm from above all else the reincarnation of sickness and sin.

The needle always injected in me in the ER, was Haldol. I often had to be held down or in restraints when they would give me the shot, because it feels like being raped. That's what it felt like for years. But in subsequent years, I believed I was a martyr. Taking the shots for the babies. Screaming at the top of my lungs "Stop Killing Babies!!!" I believed I controlled the birth orders somehow by even the way the intake process was. Birth date, height, weight, certificate, foot prints, finger prints, photo...no, no, no.... that's the intake at the jails and prisons! But since our life's sentences are soul debts that have already been set and pronounced for this life, and judgements have been made for all souls, the line up at the court house in 2014 was a tradeoff. I was given 8 years total for stalking which I think according to my past is a light sentence... because we are all trading places to get to ConCord. We all have soul debts.

I remember the day I told the judge "Who do you think you are talking to?" I was held apart in court and taken away in a cop car to psych. That day I was the judge! I particularly also remember a day in which I stood before the court as the "Creator of Abortion." I stood judgement for that in a hell realm. All that was evil was pinned on me as I stood before a modern day judge. But why? Because I am mother earth's seed. The seed of Eve. An ancient soul, which has repeated so many times, this life is just a process of walking out an accumulation soul debts, as well as

giftings. *šemiṭṭa* means to cancel a debt in Hebrew. We are all last souls cycling through, cancelling our debts. A great inheritance awaits, where we all cross over as one into ConCord. All humans have an inheritance of great measure. The World Wide Web is the way it is tracked currently, but in the spirit world it is all calculated and fair. Down to the last dotted I. Sin is no more.

I believe sin to be in the seed of reproduction, so it is parallel to good. I believe that God and Satan are like brothers both symbolically and literally they are a part of each other, and one does not come without the other. Why pin everything bad on a fallen angel, and exactly why do we have such an enemy is my question??? Only to avail that there is evil on this earth, and it comes in the form of sex. Just take a look around at the pornography in our society. That does not exist in ConCord. Everyone is whole and pure sexually, and there is no such thing as molestation or rape. I once saw a vision of sperm swimming upstream like salmon. At first and generationally there was survival of the fittest. The weak became strong and fought along side each other as warriors. There was always a leader, but the leader shifted…so as to pull in the flanks of all the souls that needed to be accounted for, which was down to the last cell. I liken a cell to a jail cell. Or a "sale" of goods. A flash of fresh cells at the market where you sell your kidneys and such. In the sperm battle it was noticed the sickness and frailty of the weaker ones and they went to breed with the healthy females, because they needed the virility. This was also a vision in jail that every 6th generation there is a female that correlates the family's genetic coding, to be pure. This is the Illuminati, or Masons I believe. Adam is actually a very talented brick mason so that really played a part in my attraction

Some of Adam and Eve's children were twins. Twinning is important to my psychosis. Both Cain and Abel were twins with females. Abel's was Jumella, and Cain's was Aclima. I had this thought come to me in prison while writing and I wondered if it was true and googled it when I got out and it was! This leads me to believe in twin souls. Pairs of souls. Cells divided by Mitosis. All coming from one energy source, a cell. In the holding cell at the jail, I was acting out being ultra-famous as a soul. I was stripped down to nothing and needing to escape my room. I had nothing left but my face which had been traded as a disguise and an acceptably beautiful shell. I was being helped, and I saw like the Oscar's of famous people clapping for me. I remember Brad Pitt and Ellen DeGeneres mostly, but it was a crowd in a tv screen watching my performance in the holding cell. I could slip under the door if the timing was right, and I peaked out into the office area and was shape shifting and moving people and objects around to my pleasure. Everyone that came into booking was trading places to get to ConCord. I saw my old boss's granddaughter coming in for me in cuffs, she must of only been 15. But she her virginity would never be raped. She had been saved from that. I copied motions and set the clock. For hours upon upon hours I played this out. Seeing writing on the doors and walls and it was all meant as clues. The clues all lead back to the Reincarnation Center, and I had an important job to do. Connect the soul pairs. Watch every move. Be ready....I was tortured, almost drowned, almost suffocated holding my breath as I did a backwards bend to squeeze under the door, and hide everything but my face, I was trading a sentence with a man. I had to be a man, basically. I had to walk those shoes, once or twice! I am a Black Fox female. I am native to this land, and I have fierce battled for my "right to remain silent." I believe we are all under life sentences, soul debts calculated. All performers headed for the Great Divide.

Chapter 2

In Wyoming on Sunday October 29th , 1978, Jacob Shelby Black was born a whopping 10 pound future foot ball player. This date is important. It was also a Sunday and only one moon cycle after my birthday. Twenty-eight days. By moon I mean menses, or a woman's cycle for bearing children. I visioned once that I had been a young girl weaving a loom, counting my days until fertility. Weaving in and out counting, counting, never ceasing until I became a woman in time. Our birthdays have much meaning in the Jewish Calendar. I researched this in a book in jail and all the numbers added up to cross paths over and over in lifetimes. The numbers matched. Dates and prophecy and my birth is actually a day of an ancient Jewish Feast, Tishrei.

I would trade a billion times and items to get to Jake by February of 2019. It was February 10th, 2019 on a blustery winters day. I had been staying at the shelter because I was too much for my parents and I had been evicted, and kicked off the

Section 8 program. It was winter cold out and I was searching for Jake around downtown. We weren't allowed to stay in the shelter all day, and it was a Sunday. Most everything down town was closed. I don't remember exactly what I was doing before I went into the Cricket Clothing Company near Broadway. Broadway is a thriving business street in our downtown. It is where I went to "pee in a cup," for 22 months while I was in the Mental Health Treatment Court with Judge Kolar. This day was February 10th, and I ended up being arrested for trespass on the hospital.

I always played at the hospital. It was such a game. That day I had traded some items at the Cricket Clothing Company. I had actually just stolen some "Montana Last Best Place," t-shirts and some napkins with foxes on them. I talked candidly to the cashier as I stole and walked right out like I owned the place. The connection there was that I had had a black neighbor that was always trying to get me onto Cricket Wireless. He is the one who gave me the seashell necklace I wore around my neck as protection for years! I believed I could hear the spiritual realm through it, or it was deeply connected to who I am. I wouldn't want to remove it when I would go to the ER or jail. The necklace was such a symbol and left it in a purse the day I was arrested, February 10th, 2019. Please remember that February 11th is my repeating date for so much. Nothing is coincidence in ConCord.

In 2013 I came into the jail with nothing hidden in me but a hair tie. My contraband was a hair tie in my secret lock box of a vagina??? It only made sense to me years later when in a sequence I needed to bind and loose with my hair. I did in fact shortly before being arrested cut off all my hair to trade for Jake. I was laughing and cutting it off, I was so happy and thrilled to have traded even my hair for him. My snaky hair, my binding and loosing hair. What you come in with you don't come out with in the preorganized system of trades. Hair. Shave that head then boy. A shave and a haircut in psych. A piss in a cup, and vital signs. Hair is biblically a protection, and Samson was strong because of his hair. Imagine the world spectrum of disorders is actually found in hair. DNA strands, and we can all morph. I know my heritage is native as I have actually seen my freckles blending into one smooth color of skin. This happened while someone was drawing my blood. I often have dreams that my blood is extremely important to ConCord, and there are always people who attempt to take my blood from me.

That Sunday afternoon I also went to the Brew Pub. I had just skipped off in glee from the Cricket Clothing Store with my gifts for Jake. I went into the Brew Pub and ordered a glass of wine for me, and a beer for Jake, and sat there and waited. I was trying to trade the things I had just taken from the clothing store. An older couple walked in and I thought they needed the Last Best Place shirts. In the meantime my alcohol was taken by the bar tender, and they asked me to leave. I am proud to say I have paid back both those places in amends! I went out and wandered some more on my quest. I ran into two cops, one was someone I knew from High School. Brad something or other. I told them of my quest and they just laughed. Brothers always work in teams. It is who to trust and when that is important to me. Good cop, bad cop.

I next went to an open house for a condo in a building by the hospital. I acted like I wanted to buy it. Just part of the sequence at this point. I had started my period and had nothing for it. I left the toilet unflushed, I do believe as I left the scene. I was very inconsiderate, and believe I was acting out a ER scene, utilizing this condo. All my specimens need to be collected and kept somehow. I then left and headed toward the hospital which seemed very appropriate to my next move, plus it was freezing out. I went in to the cafeteria and grabbed a sammich. They always give you sammiches in the ER and I was trying to do the hospital backwards this time. There was a man playing the piano in seating area and I danced up to him leaving all my stuff at a table, including my purse. This was a ploy to have my purse taken backwards to psych. To have everything accounted for in the Reincarnation Center. My seashell necklace was in the purse...along with ID and money. Down to the last cent everything made sense that I was coming into the hospital backwards. Stealing the sammich. I was acting out as if I was in the ER and my every move was accounted for. I wandered up to the NICU area…up the stairs and into a locked door area. I sat there for a moment and contemplated my boys and c-sections and the want of having more children. I flipped through their informational handouts and began to cry. A gal walked in the small area and put the code into the NICU door. I didn't try to follow her I was just in my own little world of pain and remorse.

I jumped up and went out of the room, this is when I believe special forces were called and suddenly I was being followed by about 6 staff of the hospital down the corridor towards the Er, but on the second floor of course. They had me arrested and I later found out that they thought I was trying to "steal a baby." Now they have me stating that I was "trying to steal a baby…" somehow in all there paperwork and statements a cop had me saying that to him. Now I know for a fact that was not even in the nearest in my mind what I was doing near the NICU. I was crying over my own children and it had zero to do with an attempt to trade or steal a baby. This was swept under the rug in court and never mentioned again, until I saw it on paperwork in the prison.

I was taken to jail where I heavily hallucinated in the holding cell. I saw movies on the floor of Rainbow Bridges crossing from city to city, from realm to realm. The dead coming back in other shells. I also had nothing for my period and blood was getting everywhere, I was naked. I began to use it to write on the walls, clues. Something had to connect to get me out of there. When food was brought to me, I knew I needed it in trade. Some went down the toilet to the Nether World and some was saved to give to whoever would be trading me. This was the time I visioned every sixth generation spiritually mating. Coming into the jail cell to trade me faces was Adam. I have a bazillion older brothers in the spirit world and we are all a team fighting for the good. Split between male and female. Half souls searching for our final mates. Wolves. Foxes. The living and the dead, generationally connected with a secret.

Somewhat of a time machine relaying the beginning to the end. One long tunnel message. All born in order, all factually eternal, but keep being born to earth over and over. Its like walking into a room, and knowing the answer to a question, in mid conversation because you have lived that sequence before. I believe that this all has happened in 40 years of God's time and that we can connect the beginning and end, very rapidly now. It's found in branding. For example; Russell brands make the prison clothing. We own Russell Brand, and these are like business suits for ConCord. Alpha men and women. The ones that actually get behind walls. We own the rights to the first coffee bean and that is such a luxury in the jails and is traded. If you think how much money is made from fancy coffee, imagine being the inheritor of the first coffee bean, in the Garden of Eden. How far back would you have to go to be the first to discover the bean, and what it does!!! The spiritual inheritance of every soul to walk this planet is already decided and commodities are waged for their namesakes. Branding and teams. I also identify as being the first blue eyed baby. Therefore, I own rights to the color blue. The sky.

The ocean. Blue cop lights...anything blue is my inheritance and my generations. Sapphires. Cigarettes and drugs are contraband but are also sold and traded just as fast. Everything is valuable and part of this game.

In a dream I had repeatedly soul pairing and dating was shown. The trick to soul dating is you can be beautiful and alluring, but not have sex with the person that is not your soul mate. You are ultimately connected to this soul, and nothing will appease until you find each other. Other souls in ConCord are there to teach you things, as well as in Flatt. You can sing and dance and entice one that is not your soul mate, as they line up to match in a pattern, but much like an alphabet in order we are all in order and matched in the end. A with A and One with One. There is a battle over this. There is in fact a force so strong trying to fight the matching of souls. That is why often I hear warriors fighting over the airwaves in the spirit world. Everyone is ready to cross over.

So the way intake is in the prison is that you have a mugshot and fingerprints and they account for your tattoos and scars. Scars and tattoos are also spiritually driven. Every accident we have ever had that left a scar was from another life. I have tons of scars in this life from being run over by a car at 19, c-sections and skin cancer. I trade in skin at this point. Down to the last cell, and breath I have traded. All for the revelations of ailments, to be traded for healthy and whole offspring. There is also no such thing as homosexuality in ConCord. Every soul is either male or female, and all the confusion of Flatt is gone. We are beautiful and whole, and we exchange healthy cells like a transfusion, as we reincarnate. The mugshots and finger prints are simply tracking spiritual processes. They are completely unnecessary in the scheme of things, but document all soul debts, none the less. I drew this rainbow spectrum in the prison. And just think of the range of human ailments, including accidents that have accumulated at this point. Everything under the sun...accounted for and brought to fruition in this generation.

A Poem... "Somewhere, Awake..."

This plexiglass, this phone.

The plexiglass is in a square, all around me.

The phone cord is severed…no one is listening.

I hear a dial tone out in space,

makes me think there is a chance it could be you.

There's a bazillion faces walking by my plexiglass.

I am checking to see if any are familiar.

They walk by, one by one.

Lined up.

No.

No.

Not you.

Next.

Nope.

Not.

More faces.

No. Next. Not.

Operator standing by.

Black, Wake up.

My emergency is…Black won't wake up!

I am stuck here in my plexiglass screaming.

Black, wake up!

The cord is severed and the realms cannot speak.

I am a black man in a cell.

Alone.

And I wake up, Black.

After the first drunken black out.

Black.

And White.

Plexiglass.

Trade me places?

Sit here.

Trade me places?

You make the call!

Black. Wake up. You''ll be late for practice.

We never actually had to practice.

When life means inevitable death.

What would you want in your cell?

Chapter 3

I remember a dream sequence I had in the psych ward. I know I was dreaming but at the end of my dream it was a coach of some sort telling Jake to WAKE UP! I immediately jumped out of my bed and requested to see Jake's obituary online. I didn't believe he was dead at all. He is very much with me. Another dream I had Martin Luther King

Jrs' voice inside me and I was speaking to a large auditorium, sparsely filled with families. I came out as a white woman and there were people of all cultures in the crowd. I was very intimidated until I realized that I was speaking in MLKs voice, and I was trusted. At the end of the dream it said remember 12 o'clock....remember 12 o'clock. When I awoke I googled when MLK died and Google said 12:01. Now I looked it up again on the internet and it has changed! What profound dreams to experience, and no its not weird for things in the past to change. It is called the Mandella Effect.

The "Ourglass" sifts and sorts who knows what, at what time as we connect in serendipitous manners. There are realms and layers letting souls/shells crossover between ConCord and Flatt. It happens faster than the internet and is like a back and forth heartbeat between souls crossing in and out. Bipolar is a split in the soul. A split ego per se', between two rhythms There is a percentage of male versus female traits that are genetically driven from the beginning of time. The trade is for genetics and is a spiritual process to keep the Army balanced between rich and poor. Except we are all in fact very well inherited, though in this life it may seem desperate. The deeper the soul tie, the more is inherited and blessed upon, and I believe that Jake and I are pretty high up there as famous soul mates. Much like Star Wars the end is matching us all to the beginning, and I am Miranda Black. A black maiden in a white women's body. I do recall having to climb the stairs in my castle as a maid a time or two! Up and down those stairs, have been whipped, and scrunched over stoves, and toilets scrubbing for ions! I've been a slave a lot!

I have a memory of being on a slave ship. This was very intense and terrifying as I was being used as a young concubine. The men did not want to get there wive's pregnant in the ships undercarriage, so they would choose one female to sleep with. In this memory I was told to stay quiet and stay down so they would not pick me, by my mother. I remember this as a past life and the smell of the ship even. Rancid food, vomit and stench of death. This was an extremely unpleasant memory to have, had and I was catatonic with fear. I often got catatonic because of fear in psychoses.

To end this chapter, I am going to share something I wrote many years ago, I do believe right during the time I had been to jail initially in 2013. I had started more of a fictional book to delve out of memoir style, and a lot of my themes were of pirates, and widow's peaks of moonlight madness.

NEVER FORGET OURGLASS

OUR SIGN AND SYMBOL

WHAT YOU WILL...

YOU WILL

FIND IN A CELL

YOU ARE THE APPLE

OF MINE EYE'S

"Pirates Melody"

With a broken heart Tajse continued into the world until he met a fair-haired women in the North. They wed and twins were born. The boy, blonde, had blue eyes...one which was a weak and lazy eye. The girl was a fiery red head with green eyes and she grew up to be a mad woman everyone called a witch. She married a wealthy man, simply because she was beautiful, and had two raven haired little boys. A few years later she was burned at the stake for heresy, by her own husband who did not understand her rants of religion and purity of importance.

She was the beginning of the bloodline to eventually become Clark Son's. Of her brother with the lazy eye? HE was of the New House of Order and bore all girls, seven to be exact, and one of these fine young ladies happened to marry a pirate.

And with young Melody Raposa traveled a note. That had been passed down from her grandfather Tajse'. The note traveled the world and if you can imagine a ship full of robust, dark haired and tan Raposa types, then you know that Melody was one happy woman. And the family story was that of a mission. A mission from God, and she knew somehow she was vital. She was an avid reader and nearly genius. She remember that her mad aunt had been of art and talent, as well. And what they had done to her for standing out the way she did...but Melody felt safe with her husband and other wives of the crew. She dressed rather flirtatiously, in mid drift tops with long flowing skirts were the style for all the ladies on board. In exchange for her hand, and her chance to see the world, the Captain was let in on the Secret Of Life. The secret to the Game of Life, and he was told somewhere down the his descendants would own the ocean. Now what kind of pirate doesn't like the sound of that!

So you see such a clan starts out very small. Obviously red haired Mad Aunt burned at the stake doesn't get to be named, she was just one of such, of course, but the first in a line of Cross-Overs. To Melody Raposa only slightly touched by the angels, it's a world beyond worlds to think she was part of something that would one day unite the spiritual realm with the Earth in a profound, way whatever may come. Heaven on Earth. She is told through Tajse's stories that every nation and every tongue will align at once. It will be called Sketchin Destiny (Delaney-Dye Contract), and in one splendid moment of awe and shock, no one will fight and they will all understand, and every knee will bow. She looks up at the sky and throws her hands up in praise, to the one true God that has chosen her family for just such a task. She hides the note carefully, because she does not know how long it will take for this plan. Melody is ultimately fulfilled and she dances in freedom on the ships starboard quite often. No, she does not fall in the ocean and get eaten by a shark. She lives a wonderful and prosperous life, with the Raposa's. Pirates on a mission from God with the fortitude and knowledge of the ages, they will "steal" and plunder asunder all the way to until the Americas were "discovered..."

For the trick is to look real bad, but be good while you are doing it~! Because "Robin for the Hood," wasn't invented yesterday.

Chapter 4

So that story outlines my history or lineage in a "fictional sense." I am a Nehus (New House Order) and A Clark Son. It could possibly something from a past life that I don't understand yet. But somehow I knew that I would be in a cell, with an apple in 2018, which I wrote "Pirate's Melody" in 2014. I had been in the cell arrested for the first time in August of 2013 and was so excited to see the commissary note in the bag of food in holding when I experienced my first Turtle Suit. On the note it said "Homecoming." Lol, something I'd been practicing for except I thought it the jail was like heaven! I had arrived at my destination in ConCord. If you have not figured this out yet, I believe my own brain! I may be possessed with an evil spirit, I do not know, and I am sure that all my visions will come under attack in a lot of directions. I am just telling it as I have seen it and it is my story to tell. So the holding cell was a 2013 Homecoming for Adam and I. But that was not the end of the story.

I believe Adam and I are soul siblings in a family, possibly cousins or aunt and uncle, niece or nephew what have you. Just someone spiritually related and he is two years my senior in this lifetime. At one point I was also his mother, and one life he was my father. But we are related! Adam is also related to Megan Fox, the actress. They are Cross-Overs. We are all in a line up, very close to being back to our ConCord mates, the crazier the better now, as all psych and systems are hacked! I saw Eminem's signature on my wall, after hiding my soul in the best damn bed roll you ever seen between the army of prisoners waiting to be set free, and the babies waiting to be born! Just wait until it all flips on its axis and everything is exposed to the light. Lawsuits coming in since the dawn of mankind.

I just don't have a clue who all is aware of it, right at the moment, but sometimes the whole wide world knows who I am! Sometimes taking a selfie can be a mugshot because of the way we act so fast now with social media. The camera captures your soul though and don't you think that someone really did know how to make glasses or lenses because some one in the line up in the future knew there would be eyeballs? Or the wheel for example…. reinvented a lot! All the precision it takes for something to be new, yet always based on something that already existed??? ABC, 123. It starts with ONE. WON. Already laid down in cement at the beginning. By breath. By the light in the void. By the very ALPHA and OMEGA and the first thing was a word…therefore God had a voice. I think I have GOD's voice. Not face. Nor hands, nor or hair. I am a prophet??? Well, I don't know about that but in Alpha section in the jail my first three days after being arrested at the hospital I wasn't given any meds. OH boy howdy. I didn't sleep…and someone had etched on the door a beautiful woman with a crown, that had hair growing from the top of the door down the bottom. It must have taken a very long time to etch that in the door and yet I was there. Possibly in all my assumptions all such buildings are built to be a mirage, of hiding something. Especially brick masonry? Like who wants to spend all that time measuring shit when you're also the designer, the slave, the merchant, captain and a woman all at once? But I did. Hollering between walls, passing notes, making calls. For the first two weeks of jail, I was in Alpha where you only get out of your cell for an hour. Wouldn't be my last time there in that five months. So…bare naked in this cell with the etched in woman on the door. I drew cuts in the hair as a clue, and then threw every last stich of clothing out my door hole, where they serve food trays through. I wrote names and birthdates on the walls…and of course there were other clues for me all over the walls, including a lot of miniature items for my army, and plenty of food crumbs. I flooded my toilet and laid hallucinating and staring at angles and light, trying to decipher my next move. I stood on my bed and after a series of commands and reactions to the spirit world, as well, as concrete between me and my soul mate something told me I had to stand rigid and fall backwards. I could not do that. NO matter how hard I tried, I cannot trust to fall backwards, but I am afraid if I ever end up in that situation in a jail cell again, I may decide falling and being knocked out, is indeed what I am supposed to do to escape. Or reunite with Jake. Die? Risk death? Maybe...but babe I'd rather try falling backwards out of a plane with you, ya freakin pilot! Top Gun my ass, Mr. Take me on a Cruise!

I was basically doing all kinds of things with my movements and body which was playing with silhouettes and shadows and mimicking them. After first daylight I was let out my cell, and who do I see but my Flatt step cousin Paige! So she like's girls right? Well in my mind I am going to jail court with someone related to me who is badass in Alpha status. I said hi to her, and sat directly next to her in court, and this is where shit gets splicy for me. Paige does not say a word to me as we sit by each other....well at least I remember feeling quite ignored for someone I thought I was bonded with. It was almost like she was only half there, and I never saw her again during my stay. She must have bonded. This reminds me of the incidence of being with divorce contracts the same day as a good friend, Moriah and her husband...I hadn't seen in sometime. So...there is a lawyer. A judge on a video and the bailiff...or whatever. Court reporter and officer keeping track of the room. I remember I asked her if she the extremely good looking young officer who was like seeing an angel every time I saw him was her grandpa??? "Well no, that's my nephew. HUMPH. They do have the same last names! I saw him at the 406 Restaurant and he is now a cop. They were partying it up! Drunk driving? DUI, I am not sure. But it could have been a faster trip if we'd just gone the hospital to figure it out. NOT A JAIL SELL! Trust I don't watch enough TV anymore to understand the ENTIRE court room! Only when its 2013 and I think I can roll in the court and read a three-page manifesto about "why Adam is my soul mate." But still so sweet and innocent to what was going on. More will be revealed sister. A good friend, Jeff said to me once when I told him I never had the choice to lose my virginity, it was taken. He had been talking about how only pure will be first in heaven. Well turned out I am a pure in a roundabout and backwards, spiritual hipster and magnetic way! Because we exist in more than once realm.

I believe I was awake without meds for at least three days before they took me to shower. Laying in toilet water and eating the yucky bean thingee, they give people who throw their tray. Well, I threw my tray more as an offering to my angel ant size army! Just like the orange juice on the floor in the ER, they need appeased and pleasured my army!

Soon after me a supposed baby murderer for starving her child was in that room, and pregnant, again. The little girl that died, had the same birthdate as my own mother. She was from Ohio. She had thick red curly hair and ended up being my cellie a couple months down the road. I'm still not sure if she was held responsible for the death, although I did hear she was coming to the prison around the time I got out. Go figure. Another cellie in Delta I had known from the rooms. She had my nemesis name in life which is Tiffany. We are good friends though. One day I thought she was Crossing over with me and I was so excited to be meeting her brother, I was banging on the vents and yelling for freedom and Christs return. Well, that's what I believe every single time things go my way for that freaking long! A series of sequences.

I don't claim to completely understand all this but it's a start to get it on paper so that maybe someone can help me decipher some things I haven't yet. I am open to suggestions of course and will play an FBI agent or doctor on any show you'd like, as long as, I am in my real and true shell. For in Flatt I believe I've been playing the role of the harlot? Yes, I said it. But its like I'm uniting all fifty states or something through my soul ties and genealogy and believe in my mind that everyone else is doing that too. Yes, me, I do. But as far as this makes any kind of sense at all, I should let you know that I haven't even let myself think about these kinds of ideas for over a year. So, I am shifting back very slowly. I have been smoking marijuana for three months, to of little or no consequence in my mind besides feeling relaxed and a little dopey happy. Sleeping better, not paranoid, for what do I have left to be frightened of at this point? Come hell or high water I've been it all and I am ready to die if need be. The curse is that I am not allowed to end my shell. So basically, I wrote this in 2018 when I was living in my parent's basement. I came home one night with this idea....it was on my blog but I've done some editing.

Why do I have to do this in the dark? Why won't you just leave the lights on for me when I come home? Mom? Dad? Why don't you understand this at all? WHY is the irony not flabbergasting you? Have you switched places on me? I am in the basement. I am here alone (just like 18 alone on earth, no soul mate)...

I guess you could come over and we could eat Cheetos and watch HBO after midnight...did you bring the pebble Jake? NO? Adam? Nope. I left the catnip for Zander.

Well I asked via Facebook you guys! It was like a very big deal at Dehler Park or something! So, about this pebble idea? Did anyone surround the garden gates with pebbles? (Speaking of her miniatures again.)

Well, is it going to be granite or just like the boss' countertops? Because I am way excited. What if it looks like cement, will it still be worth it in the end? You know what we build with? Sticks and stones...bones? Knarly holy genes...no jeans again? LMAO. Leaving that code behind again?

Unlock my door Megan Keys. My very own sister. Sixteen years and 30 days younger than me with a mother's birthday in between. My daughter basically in Flatt during a time when a lot of young girls were paying soul debts to be blessed with healthy children in their orders. Remember men that we decided we would never fight over what would be more valuable in any given situation involving hostages in a cellar in TIM BUCK TWO!

Now boys…courage, brains, heart, we all take one. As a brother so hands over his life, so shall I. I will take courage. You will take brains, and you will take heart. Whoever is divided at this stage in the game over which side of the family they should choose?

Well, you can pick first. Lord. Have mercy.

One who said my heart was not equal to "what exactly again?" MMMMMMMMMMM…. ribs for dinner! Slice me in half! Whoever would dare to not call these lives fair? Game on. Mortal Kombat, yet again with no heroes anticlimax? What's WELL

FAIR? Free shit? Hard knock life? NO, we are the KINGS AND QUEENS of this generation, the ones that don't like to "play house" very well with the dollhouse loving crazy cat lady!

Now. Niner Niner Red Radio Flyer…. flush cats' hair down the toilet and leave some food out for Sparkly…ruby red slippers on the OLD YELLER! But I said go holler to the birds and Whisper sweet nothings to an orange Tabby, then leave your cents on the table. Glue them on the table all pretty if you must. Measure. Dammit measure. Lean over and measure the hem. On your knees…wasn't there ever to be a stowed away on the Black Pearl? Are we ever going to have another Keira Knightly? Johnny Depp and Orlando Bloom, yum, yum. OMG who's putting all that weight on these days? Any 43 years old pregnant with twins?

Who is the bait here? What's the debate? Bring your little red dagger from your shed, right? Meet me at the John son's mail box…hand deliver baby announcement this time. Say thanks for everything uncle. Go watch some more "I dream of Genie." I know you don't remember what happened because you weren't really there for that, I am sorry, you left the room. That's why I saw you walk by in the ICU Center of the hospital. That's like saying "hey I see YOU." ICU MED STAFF TO TRAUMA. Quick get Dave and the boys and make a big scene on the rims. Die faster…heal faster. Come back to Connie faster. I know she knows. Has to know he is there with her.

++
++

I am in fact in Flatt writing this, but it's bringing back a lot of memories. I do not know the true from the false and ended up going to the ER to check things out. I had a friend take me and he kept me in Flatt. I did not sing or act up…just watched the process and saw no shape shifting. Today is January 9, 2022. Something is definitely stirring in the spiritual realm though. Don't know what exactly as I am not allowed to know all at once…it's such an intriguing mystery!!!

I do know however, that my "trying to steal a baby…" was swept under the rug in court hearings, and I only discovered the accusation in writing behind prison walls. It was on my therapist's computer. Never brought up to me or talked about in court or any formal setting. So all over paper work, but never brought up in court! How strange is that?

More about prison life to come in Part 3 "Jessie the Cowgirl."